PREVIOUSLY PUBLISHED AS REGIE'S INSIGHT; FAUSTER 2015 AND REVISED IN 2017 BY KAREN DACHSEL

FAUSTER LEAVES A WELL KNOWN PLACE IN HOPES OF FINDING A NEW HOME... HIS HEART IS SADDENED WHEN HIS ONLY HOME IS FOUND LACKING THE CARE IT NEEDS, AS HE LOOKS FOR A NEW ONE HE FINDS NEW FRIENDS...... A LESSON TAUGHT ABOUT FORGIVENESS.

NEW & REVISED

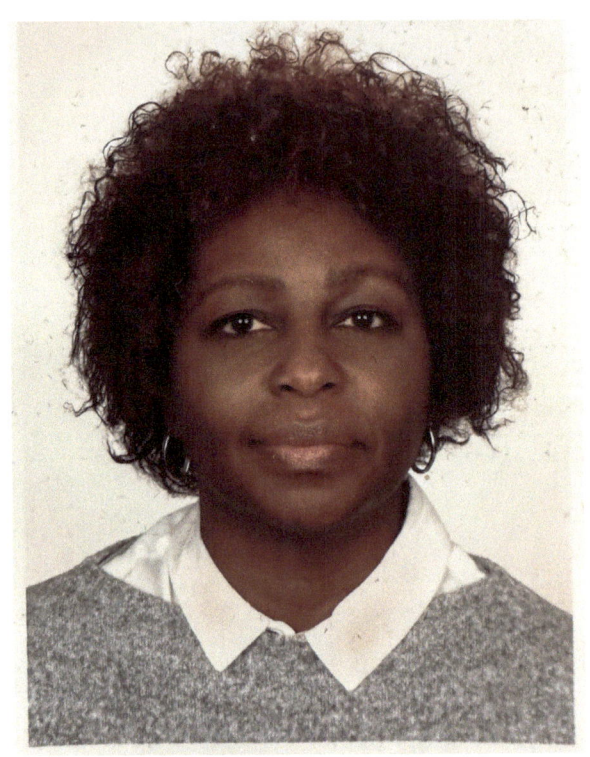

KAREN DACHSEL

A SELF PUBLISHER…. STARTED WRITING AT THE AGE OF SIX… LOVES A GOOD CUP OF CAPPUCCINO, JELLY BEANS, LICORICE, A GOOD MOVIE, A GOOD LAUGH AND HER FAVORITE IS A GOOD PRAYER…

REMEMBER WHENEVER AND WHATEVER YOU DO… MAKE THE DAY TO BRING A BLESSING TO SOMEONE ELSE!

HOPE YOU ENJOY YOUR READING!

IMPRESSUM

ALLE RECHTE AM WERK LIEGEN BEIM

AUTOR KAREN DACHSEL

REGISTERED BY ENGLISH4ALL- HAPUH'S WRITING'S

NO PART OF THIS PUBLICATION MAY BE REPRODUCED, STORED IN A RETRIEVAL SYSTEM, TRANSMITTED IN ANY FORM OR BY ANY MEANS ELECTRONIC, MECHANICAL, PHOTOCOPYING, RECORDING OR OTHERWISE WITHOUT WRITTEN PERMISSION OF THE PUBLISHER.

NIGHT WAS FALLING AND THEY DIDN'T HAVE A CLUE OF WHAT THEY WOULD SEE... THEY FOLLOWED EACH OTHER'S SHADOW... WHO COULD CLIMB UP FASTER TO THE MOUNTAIN THAN THE OTHER... HEARING WATERS FOR AFAR... RUMBLE, RUMBLE, RUMBLE, RUMBLE... WAGGLING AROUND, USING ALL OF THEIR STRENGTH TO GET TO THE TOP.

THE RAIN DEW OF SLIME FROM THE MOUNTAINS MADE THEIR HUFFS SLIPPERY TO GRIP THE DIRT... SOMETIMES SLIDING BUT MOST OF THE TIME FALLING DOWN...

"AS IF THE RACE WAS TO BE WON". SMALL STONES HURLED DOWN AS WET GRASS DUSTED THEIR FEET LIKE SOCKS, BUT THEY KEPT ON RUNNING... BREATHING FRANTICALLY AS THEY PEEPED AT EACH OTHER.

COME ON NILEY, SAID FAUSTER... YOU CAN DO IT! "PANTING HE WAS"... I'M COMING... ALMOST THERE... YEAH! YEAH!... NILEY, NILEY, WHERE ARE YOU? (NILEY WAS ON THE OTHER SIDE, WITH HIS FACE DOWN IN THE GRASS AND HIS BODY TURNED SIDEWAYS ON THE DIRT COOLING HIMSELF OFF).

NILEY, NILEY WHERE ARE YOU? WHEW, I DID... HE SAID QUIETLY... I DID... I DID IT (AFTER SEARCHING, FAUSTER FOUND NILEY LAYING UNDER A TREE SNOOZING OFF)

CAN WE DO THAT AGAIN? WHAT! ... SAID FAUSTER, YOUR MORE CRAZIER THAN I THOUGHT... THEY CHUCKLED AND RESTED, UNTIL THEY FELL ASLEEP UNDER THE TREE... (BUUUURP), NILEY AWOKE SHAKING HIS HEAD (BUUUURP)

FAUSTER LET OUT THE BIGGEST BELCH EVER.... "OPHS" SORRY...

THEIR STOMACHS SNARLED WITH PANGS OF HUNGER AS THEY WALKED BACK TO THE BARN, WHEN SUDDENLY A SMELL OF WOOD SNIPPED THEIR NOSES AND THEY HAD TO SEE WHAT THEIR SENSES COULD ALREADY TASTE (THEY FOLLOWED THE DUFT)... THE CLOSER THEY GOT THE MORE THEIR TONGUES SWAGGERED WITH MOISTNESS.

NOW THE SUMMER SEASON HAD ARRIVED AND MANY PEOPLE WERE ON VACATION CAMPING OUT... JUST ENJOYING THEMSELVES AND RELAXING... FAUSTER AND NILEY COULD SMELL THE CAMPER'S GRILLING...

THEIR EYES MET WITH THEIR TONGUES HANGING WITH DRIPS OF SALIVA DROOLING DOWN THE CRACKS OF THEIR JAWS... THEY HAD BEEN WATCHING THEIR PREY FOR OVER AN HOUR, A SUDDEN BURST OF THRASHING NOISES MADE EVERYONE DASH TO THEIR CARS, CAMPERS AND HUTS IN HOPES NOT TO GET CAUGHT IN THE RAIN..- "AND RAIN IT DID"... SO, HEAVY THAT NO ONE COULD SEE IN FRONT OF THEIR FACES...(LOUD THUNDER SOUNDS CRASHED THE AIR)

NOW, WAS THEIR CHANCE AND THEY TOOK IT... FAUSTER AND RILEY GRABBED EVERYTHING THAT THEY COULD (HOT OR COLD) AS THEY RAN AND HID UNDER THE OLD BARN HOUSE... THEY ATE SO FAST (ONLY THEIR FANGS WERE SHOWING)... THEIR STOMACHS INFLATED LIKE A TIRE BEING PUMPED... THEY WERE SO FULL... THAT THEY COULDN'T GASP ANYMORE... WHILE LICKING THEIR PAWS.

AFTER EATING THEIR EYES BECAME SO HEAVY THAT THEY CURLED UP TO TAKE THEIR NEXT NAP.

SOON AFTER THE RAIN STOPPED... THEY AWOKE AND STARTED BACK... THE MORE THEY WALKED THE MORE THEIR STOMACHS BECAME NAUSEOUS... THE BEEF STEAKS WERE MAKING THEM FEEL WEEZY... WHOA! IT WAS A GAS ATTACK... THE REEK OF COOKED BEEF SCATTERED THE AIR... THE RUMBLING BECOME STRONGER AND STRONGER... THEIR WALKING TURNED INTO A TROT AND EVERY TIME THEY HAD TO STOP... THEIR TAILS WOULD WHISK THE BRISK AWAY... THEY TROTTED AS FAST AS POSSIBLE TO GET TO THE FLOWING WATER'S...

THINKING THAT A SEAT IN THE COOLNESS WOULD HELP THEIR BODIES CALM DOWN... AAAHHH! THIS FEELS GOOD, DOESN'T IT? YEAH, SURE DOES... AS THEY WERE COOLING THEIR BODIES, THEY HEARD SOMEONE SPEAKING...

HAVEN'T SEEN YOU GUYS AROUND HERE BEFORE, (AS HE DRANK FROM THE WATER), MY NAME IS KLERT... OH, HI KLERT... MY NAME IS FAUSTER AND THIS IS NILEY... WE WERE THINKING ABOUT GOING FOR A SWIM, WELL, CAN I JOIN YOU? YEAH, I DON'T SEE WHY NOT... COME ON, THEY SHOUTED!

THEIR PLAYING AND TOSSING TURNED INTO A UNISON OF A MIDNIGHT PRANCE... AND GLADLY THEIR STOMACHS SETTLED ALONG THE WAY. THE MOON GLOWED WHILE THEY TRAMPLED...BACK AND FORTH THEY WENT, KICKING UP THEIR HUFFS. THEIR ROCKING SENT THEM THROUGH, AROUND AND UP THE MOUNTAIN SIDE... THEY SLID DOWN ONE BY ONE... FULL OF MUD AND IT FELT WARM AND OOZY TO THEIR FUR... THEY WERE HAVING SO MUCH FUN...

THAT THEY DIDN'T NOTICE THE DAY BREAKING FORTH… THE DAWN GAVE THEIR EARS THE AWAKENING TOWARDS HOME AGAIN (FOR THEY HEARD THE CRIES OF OTHER'S NEAR AND AFAR) … AS THEY MOVED TOWARD THE SOUND… TO WHAT SEEMED TO START AS A NORMAL DAY, THEIR EYES BEHELD A BLAZING BURNING WOOD… "IT WAS THE BARN HOUSE" THEY COULD SEE PEOPLE RUNNING IN EVERY DIRECTION, HURRYING TO RUSH FOR WATER… EVERYONE PITCHED IN AS FAST AS THEY COULD. THEY DASHED IN TO HELP OUT, BUT IT SEEMED HOPELESS…

THE FLAMES WERE EXPLODING FASTER THAN THE WATER WAS COMING, ALL THE CAMPER'S PITCHED IN TO GATHER THEIR REMAINS… SOON THE FIRE TRUCK CAME AND ALL THAT WAS LEFT WERE RUINS OF WHAT USED TO BE… "A BIG PILE OF ASHES"

WEEKS AFTER THE OWNERS DECIDED TO SELL THE LAND AND MOVE TO ANOTHER AREA… THEY PACKED UP AND HEADED WEST, NEVER TO RETURN…

THE GROUND WAS PURCHASED BY SOMEONE ELSE AND THE NEW OWNER HAD

THE BARN HOUSE REBUILT (THE SAME WAY IT WAS BEFORE) AND WHILE ALL THIS WAS TAKING PLACE... FAUSTER, NILEY AND KLERT WERE ROAMING AROUND JUST HAVING FUN... KIND OF MISSING THE GOOD OLE TIMES THAT THEY ONCE HAD AT THE BARN...

ONE DAY WHILE THEY WERE DRINKING BY THE RIVER, THEY MET AN OLD FRIEND BY THE NAME OF QUACKY... HE TOLD THEM ALL ABOUT THE NEW FARMER AND THEY DECIDED TO CHECK IT OUT...

WOW! WHAT THEY SAW WAS EVEN BETTER THAN BEFORE... FOR THIS WASN'T THE FIRST TIME THAT THE OLD BARN HAD BURNED DOWN...

FAUSTER RECOGNIZED THAT THE NEW OWNER WAS THE SON OF THE FIRST ORIGINAL OWNER... HE HAD BEEN TRYING TO BUY THE FAMILIES GROUND BACK... WHILE HIS FAMILY HAD LOST EVERYTHING, FIFTEEN YEARS AGO TO A BAD INVESTMENT... THE FAMILY WAS CHEATED OUT OF THEIR MONIES AND HAD TO MOVE OFF OF THEIR LAND...

THEY NEVER RECEIVED A PENNY BACK… THEIR PLAN WAS TO OPEN A RANCH HOUSE INN AND WHEN THEY PARTNERED WITH THIS INVESTMENT COMPANY… THE COMPANY SUDDENLY WENT BANKRUPT… THE SON NEVER FORGOT HOW HEART BROKEN HIS PARENT'S WERE AND PROMISED THEM THAT HE WOULD ONE DAY OWN THE LAND AGAIN…

AFTER GROWING UP, HE BECAME A BUILDER AND OPENED UP HIS OWN INVEST FIRM… VERY WEALTHY TO SAY THE LEAST, BUT HE NEVER FORGOT THE DREAM… HE WENT BACK TO HIS HOME TOWN AND PURCHASED

THE LAND...MAKING SURE THAT THE EXACT SAME PLAN AND INSTRUCTIONS FROM BEFORE WAS USED...

YOU SEE FAUSTER TOLD HIS FRIEND'S... HE ALWAYS HAD A BELIEF... FAUSTER WOULD SEE THE FAMILY SPEND TIME TOGETHER & PRAY TOGETHER... AND HE EVEN GAVE ONE OF THE PEOPLE FROM THE COMPANY A JOB AT HIS FIRM.... WHY DO YOU THINK THAT? ASKED KLERT... SIMPLE SAID FAUSTER... HE FORGAVE THEM!

FAUSTER AND HIS FRIENDS, NEVER HAD TO LEAVE THE GROUND AGAIN... FOR HE KNEW THAT THERE WAS ALWAYS FRIENDSHIP THERE... IT BROUGHT SOMETHING NEW TO ALL THEIR LIVES!

CHECK TO SEE IF YOU CAN NAME THESE FOUR IMAGED ANIMALS THAT LIVE ON A FARM... THEN AFTER NAME THE COLORS...

www.ingramcontent.com/pod-product-compliance
Lightning Source LLC
Chambersburg PA
CBHW040031050426
42453CB00002B/83